Setting Sail!

The Family Workbook

Emily G. Hervey

Supporting Healthy International Family Transitions

Setting Sail: The Family Workbook

ISBN-13: 978-0-9852917-0-9

Chandler, AZ

Table of Contents

Introduction

Where Did This Start?

It was an early morning as the small airplane descended into the steppes of Central Asia. I was exhausted on the last leg of the journey, after our family of seven faced the multiple officials in the Russian airport. Following the arguments over checking the many suitcases we were bringing to our new home, we were the last ones to board the plane. The remaining empty seats were scattered down the aisle, and as I sat down, I realized mine did not have a seatbelt attached. It was an almost ironic demonstration of a missing piece of security, not just the physical mechanism, but the violation of the norms to which I was accustomed. What would be unacceptable in the Western world was of no concern here. As the plane landed, we approached a city full of Soviet-style apartment buildings, yet interwoven with a culture from a nomadic heritage. It was new setting altogether. What remained constant throughout the transition was a primary aspect of life: my family.

I grew up in multiple countries and cultures across three continents, a lifestyle full of mobility. My experience helped me to learn first-hand what was helpful and what was lacking in the process of transitions. Since then, I've found ways to support individuals and families in cross-cultural settings. But after observing a variety of organizations sending families overseas, I noticed that very few included interaction between parents and children in the preparation process. While some had excellent programs in place for children and a variety of training available for adults, few activities were done as a whole family. A number of organizations recognized the value of families, but did not have a means of integrating that awareness into the established preparation process. There appeared to be an unmet need.

What's so Important about Families?

Entering a new country includes a complete change in lifestyle, surroundings, culture, community, and many other facets of life. That much change can be difficult for anyone, especially when other sources of support are also left behind. However the family is always present, and hopefully is always a place to find support. This constant makes developing a healthy and resilient family structure a key aspect of the preparation process. When describing research done on family resilience, Froma Walsh states, "How a family confronts and manages a disruptive experience, buffers stress, effectively reorganizes itself, and moves forward with life will influence immediate and long-term adaptation for every family member and for the very survival and well-being of the family unit."[1] (See Appendix B for more on family resilience.)

Think of the family as a ship. Getting ready for departure is more than training the captain and mapping the course. It is critical that the ship itself is in good condition, without loose pieces or leaky wood. It is also important the whole crew knows how to work together, especially if they face any storms. Without those two factors, as soon as the ship hits choppy waters, it might start sinking without a crew who knows how to fix it!

In the same way, if a family is not built on a strong foundation, there is a greater risk for more complications when challenges arise. With no effective ways to support each other, family members struggle with anxiety and tension. Instead, developing healthy family interactions can lessen the negative effects of stress.[2] The family remains the primary constant in the midst of complete transition. The significance of that role as a source of security makes it essential to assess the coping strategies and relationships within a family. Healthy relationships help ensure they are ready to adjust in a new context.

Using the Workbook

This workbook is designed to help prepare whole families for cross-cultural transition. It takes on a holistic model, emphasizing not only individual needs, but also growth in the family unit. The model includes interaction between parents and children

---

[1] Walsh, F. (1998). *Strengthening family resilience*. New York: The Guilford Press.
[2] Walsh, p. 20, 1998

through a variety of activities and discussions. The process of going through the activities together is just as important as the content discussed. Interaction between family members often reveals areas of strengths and weaknesses in the relationships. While no family can be perfect, addressing problems before departure may be helpful to prevent further damage down the road.

The main purpose of this resource is to equip the family on emotional, relational, and spiritual levels. Families may be well-prepared on a logistical level through their sponsoring organization, but in order to thrive they need to create family processes that promote resilience.[3] In a survey of 191 parents who did missionary work overseas, 72% concurred with the statement that, "Family life education would be helpful if given before the field assignment."[4] The workbook will hopefully provide some of that insight into family life, whether used independently or in partnership with an organization.

The format and content of the program take many factors into consideration. When creating a program integrating multiple age groups, it can be helpful to have a visual analogy that can be interpreted in varying degrees of complexity. An interactive approach leads to higher retention of information. Research shows people remember about 10% of what they read, 50% when both seeing and hearing information, and up to 90% when actively doing something.[5] With this in mind, this workbook is designed to parallel characteristics of a ship, which can be seen as symbolic of movement and transitions. In years past, most people moving overseas would have travelled by boat, experiencing a much longer journey. The intermediary period was in some ways beneficial, allowing more time to grieve their losses and process imminent changes during their time between leaving "home" and entering their new environment. Today's advanced system of transportation shortens travel time, making it even more necessary to make a conscious effort to facilitate the transition process. This program provides one approach to active preparation for such transitions.

---

[3] Walsh, 1998

[4] Kruckerberg, J., & Stafford, A. (1988). The missionary's need for family life training. In K. O'Donnell, & M. O'Donnell (Eds.), *Helping missionaries grow: Readings in mental health and missions* (pp. 176-185). Pasadena, CA: William Carey Library.

[5] Knell, M. (2001). *Families on the move: Growing up overseas and loving it!* London: Monarch Books.

Suggestions for Families

Families preparing to move internationally come from a wide range of backgrounds and are travelling to a huge variety of destinations. There is also great deal of variation between organizations or churches sending them. This workbook is not specific to one organization or destination. It is designed for you as parents to lead the family in understanding the content through the activities and discussions included. You know your kids better than anyone else, and can always tailor activities and discussions to fit a wide variety of ages. However, the recommended age range is 6 to 12 years old. Children younger than that may have difficulty grasping many of the concepts introduced. On the other end, teenagers may view some activities as too simplified and less relevant for them.

The workbook is broken down into seven sections. Each section relates to one aspect of an analogy: A family is like a ship. You will have a chance to discover how the family unit, with its unique parts and united functioning, compares to a ship getting ready for departure. The workbook is created for sections to be used in chronological order, as many concepts or activities build upon what was already done or discussed. The space provided to record thoughts and questions is also purposefully included. Using that space can later provide you with reminders of specific steps that have already been planned and allow you to see areas of growth.

As a family you can choose to set aside a specific amount of time to go through the workbook, such as allotting one week for each section. It can be very challenging to not get distracted when fitting it into an already established schedule. Thus it is helpful to set specific goals and schedule times to spend together as a family. A pattern of weekly "family time" can be continued after finishing the workbook, a way to promote healthy relationships. It is also important to be aware that the closer you get to departure, the busier life will get. If you are hoping to finish the whole workbook before leaving, starting at least six months before you plan to leave will allow the needed time without feeling rushed at the end. It will also give you time to practice what you've learned before entering the brand new environment.

Recommendations for parents:

1. Before starting look over the whole workbook to get an idea of the topics covered and the resources available. Some activities require a bit more preparation, especially arranging a dinner for Part 6.

2. Each section starts with a Bible verse. As parents you are of course free to use it however you like, but you are encouraged to include prayer and the Bible throughout the process. This use of Scripture may include memorizing part of all of the verse together or talking about how it fits with what you are learning. It can be a way to remember how God's word fits with the ideas discussed. Before starting the workbook, talk about how you want to use Bible verses as a family.

3. Read each section before using it with your family. It helps to know how the topics fit with the activities. There are some discussions that are just for you as parents, and others for the whole family. Most activities require some basic preparations such as gathering materials or deciding who will give directions.

4. Be flexible. Different age children will need different levels of guidance and explanation. Make sure to allow time for questions. Young children may not understand abstract ideas or may find discussions uninteresting. Much of what you say the first time will be forgotten, but when issues come up again in the future you can look back on the activities and use them as reminders. On the other end, if you are including adolescents they may find some examples over-simplified. Allow them to focus on what is most relevant to them and give them space to engage without feeling pressured.

5. Be realistic. Children have a limited attention span and may not do best covering a whole section in one sitting. Different children will respond differently to activities. While it is great for each to have room to talk, some may not be as ready, willing, or able to express everything vocally.

6. Be observant, but not intrusive. Notice the times and topics that bring reactions, good or bad. At the same time, don't expect children to be able to explain those reactions. Some may withdraw if they feel pressured to talk.

When to Seek Help

While this workbook can be completed independently, it is very important that parents recognize when outside support is needed. There are two factors to consider: relational issues and individual concerns. If you notice that your family is having difficulty communicating or cooperating, it may be time to consult a mental health professional. Couples and/or family therapy can be very beneficial to address issues prior to departure. The workbook also includes chances to express emotions and questions. While some degree of uncertainty is normal, if a family member is showing high levels of anxiety or signs of depression, it is very important to address those concerns. Exploring those with the help of a counselor or psychologist now can prevent greater problems down the road.

Warning signs for Depression and Generalized Anxiety

• Difficulty concentrating, remembering details, and making decisions • Fatigue and decreased energy • Insomnia, early-morning wakefulness, or excessive sleeping • Irritability, restlessness • Feelings of hopelessness and/or pessimism • Feelings of guilt, worthlessness, and/or helplessness • Aches or pains, headaches, cramps, and/or digestive problems that do not ease with treatment • Overeating or appetite loss • Loss of interest in activities once pleasurable • Persistent sad, anxious, or "empty" feelings	• Excessive, ongoing worry and tension • An unrealistic view of problems • Restlessness or a feeling of being "edgy" • Trouble falling or staying asleep • Irritability • Nausea • Sweating • Muscle tension, headaches • The need to go to the bathroom frequently • Difficulty concentrating • Trembling • Being easily startled

Finally, some families have children or adolescents that are opposed to the idea of going overseas. Proceeding without addressing this concern could have negative effects on family relationships. When adolescents are forced to go against their will it might even contribute to rebellion and bitterness. Sometimes opposition might come from false ideas about the experience. Other times they might have valid concerns. In both cases it is important to assess the strength of resistance and the reason behind it. Having children talk with a third party, such as a counselor, can be a good way to get a more complete view of the problem. In some cases it might be necessary to consider postponing departure.

Suggestions for Organizations

Although this workbook is designed to be used independently by families, churches and organizations are free to implement it into their own preparation process. This use of the program may be on an individual level, partnering with each family as they prepare for transition. It can also be easily adapted to use with groups of families, with activities and discussions being guided by staff in the training programs or an outside source. Any organization or church sending out missionaries can modify the program to fit pre-existing approaches to pre-field training or use it as the starting point for preparing families to enter new cultures.

There are some benefits of creating a family training time that is set apart from what orientation they might receive from a church or organization. First, it reduces the overwhelming amount of information that is processed during a relatively short period of time. Second, it provides the opportunity for families to be more open, with the assurance that they are not being evaluated by their agency. This program can facilitate both interaction within the family and interactions among families, facilitating relationship-building among individuals while building mutual understanding in multiple aspects of life.

The modular structure makes it possible to use the program in a variety of settings. One possible format for its use would be a week-long program for a group of families preparing to move overseas, using one section each day. For this structure, it would be beneficial to include devotions and other fun activities, then allow free time to avoid it becoming too intense and tiring. It would also be very valuable to have a psychologist or counselor available to address issues that might surface and provide consultation for individuals, couples, and families. Although such a program would require setting aside an entire week of one's time, it would also remove distractions and focus on the family's upcoming transitions.

A second possible format would spread the course over seven weeks, meeting once a week and using the intermediate time for applying the skills and concepts introduced into practice. In this approach, it would be helpful to allow time for debriefing how the previous weeks have gone and what areas for further growth have been identified. The benefit of this approach is that the tools introduced can be actively integrated into daily life, with more opportunity to reflect on the resulting health of family structure and interactions. The challenge is to overcome the competition of daily responsibilities and events for time and attention during these weeks of preparation.

I would strongly encourage sending churches and organizations to consider setting apart time for families to learn together what they are going to encounter and to gain helpful strategies for engaging in their upcoming transitions. Please note that this is designed as a supplement, not a replacement, for other training available. Other needs, such as care for the individual and the couple, should also be addressed outside of this program. In addition, while it may reveal some relational issues already in place, it cannot be expected to solve all current problems. Instead, it may be helpful in identifying needs for further pastoral or professional assistance.

Final Thoughts

Regardless of how this workbook is used, I hope and pray that you will keep God at the center of the process. He made us and called us to follow Him, and for some families that means moving to foreign lands. It is vitally important to rely on and cling to Him throughout the process of transition.

Part 1: Identity

What is Our Ship Like?

"May the God who gives endurance and encouragement give you a spirit of unity among yourselves as you follow Christ Jesus, so that with one heart and mouth you may glorify the God and Father of our Lord Jesus Christ. Accept one another, then, just as Christ accepted you, in order to bring praise to God."
Romans 15: 5-7

Think about ships: Each is unique in shape, size, color, material, and many other components. They have many parts that must all work together to function well, such as the sail, the wheel, and the rudder, and different crew members that all play important roles. All the parts and people must work together to get where they want to go. They must cooperate especially when facing challenges like storms. Ships are made to go from one place to another, but while what is around them can change dramatically, the ship itself stays fairly constant. In the same way, families moving to a new culture will see a lot of differences around them, but can maintain stability within the family. It is important to make sure a family is "well-built" before sending it out, or "resilient" enough to reach that destination in good condition.

How do we make sure that we have a well-built ship?

 Good relationships are what hold you together and make you a strong family. Everyone in your family has to work together, like a crew, and each member needs to know how important he or she is to that crew. A big part of this program is helping all members of your family figure out where they fit and appreciate the roles of everyone else. This awareness is one step toward building a strong vessel.

Parents: This discussion is a chance to talk to the whole family about the illustration of a ship and what it means for them. Writing down thoughts can be helpful later when thinking back on the discussion. A picture is provided on the next page for younger children to color while you have the discussion.

Points to Ponder: The Ship

- What comes to mind when you think of a ship? What function does it serve?

_____

_____

_____

_____

_____

- Ships can't function alone and have many different parts. What are some of the various aspects of a ship?

_____

_____

_____

_____

_____

- How is a ship like a family in transition?

_____

_____

_____

_____

_____

- Think about how both ships and families from one place to another. Both have multiple parts and roles in order to function well. The different parts have distinct characteristics. All parts stay in one group throughout the transition.
- Other questions and thoughts:

_____

_____

_____

_____

What makes our family unique?

Just like ships, every family is unique, but families don't often think about what makes them who they are. While a ship is often described by what it looks like on the outside, what is also important is how well it was built, how it runs, and the places it has journeyed. In the same way, families are more than names and appearances. What your family believes, how you are organized and work together, what you value the most, your own cultural background, and the memories you have made together are all important components of who they are. Often families don't think about some of those pieces of their identities.

Activity: Family Flag

Objectives: To work together to discover important parts of your family's identity. To create a unified view of the family unit and to allow each member to describe what he or she values.

Materials: Paper, markers, magazines, scissors, glue, other decorations, wooden or plastic stick (flag pole)

Description: Your family will together create a flag that serves as a symbolic representation of your identity, including relationships, history, culture, values, beliefs, traditions, goals, interests, etc.

Directions:

- Brainstorm together as a family on what makes you who you are as a family. Create a list of important values, traditions, interests, objects, etc. What makes your family unique? What do you share in common with each other? Make sure all members have a chance to contribute to the list.

_____

_____

_____

_____

_____

_____

_____

_____

- Take the white paper and use it to design a flag that displays the most important aspects of who you are as a family. You can use pictures, words, colors, symbols, and any other creative forms of representation. If you have magazines you can cut out words or pictures from them. Get creative with any media you have!

- Mount your flag on its pole. If there are other families or friends present , explain the difference meanings of what is on your flag.

Example family flag

What stays consistent?

At the same time, think about why you decided to move in the first place. Is everyone in the family on the same page, with a common vision? Sharing that vision, especially with your children, provides a stronger sense of purpose and basis for supporting one another. Having a strong set of common beliefs as a foundation for decision-making adds a sense of security and well-being. A family can also look at more practical ways to keep life feeling consistent. Keeping patterns formed in areas like chores and routines for meals and bedtimes can help new settings feel less confusing. Families can also choose some "portable roots" to take with them wherever they go. As a family, you can identify what traditions are most important to you and what objects—such as a favorite toy or a memory book—make a place feel like home. Changes still come, and being able to adapt is very important. At the same time, keeping some things that feel familiar can help as each person adjusts.

Points to Ponder:

It's helpful to have some things remain constant for the individual and the family in the midst of transition, such as routines, responsibilities, traditions, and objects.

- What do each of you find important in the nature of your family? Every one can give their top 4-5 ideas.

_____

_____

_____

_____

_____

_____

_____

- Why are these important to you?

_____

_____

_____

_____

_____

- Parents: Which of these can continue anywhere you go? How can other ones be adapted to a new location?

_____

_____

_____

_____

_____

- Kids: Are there any other questions you have?

_____

_____

_____

_____

_____

_____

_____

- As a family come up with a statement that declares your beliefs, goals, and priorities.

_____

_____

_____

_____

_____

Who stays consistent?

Another area that is important to maintain is the relationships. It helps to identify which friends and relatives can make an effort to keep in touch, whether by mail, phone, e-mail, Skype, or any other communication resources. In times of stress it makes a difference to know that someone is there for you, helping you feel less lonely and more supported.

Points to Ponder:

- While overseas, it is very important to continue receiving support from the home culture, maintaining strong relationships with friends and relatives, and staying updated with the current trends.
- These relationships will provide a sense of constancy and care, and they can even facilitate a smoother reentry later on. Why do you think that is?

_____

_____

_____

_____

_____

- What are the important relationships in your lives that you want to maintain?

_____

_____

_____

_____

_____

- What steps can you to take in order to remain in contact with these people?

_____

_____

_____

_____

_____

_____

What makes each member unique?

A ship's crew would not work well if everyone was trying to do the same job. Each person has a unique personality and different skills and talents. It is important to appreciate those differences, knowing that God made each person to be the way he or she is supposed to be. A person's worth comes from within. Without knowing that, entering a time a brand new place can be difficult when feeling different from everyone around you. Suddenly, you are "foreign" in a different culture, with a lot of learning to do about what is normal there. It helps to have a family, reminding one another that they are accepted and loved.

Activity: Message in a Bottle

Objectives: To identify key aspects of identity and the unique nature of each member of your family. To receive mutual affirmation from family members, strengthening self-esteem and communicating inherent self-worth. This affirmation allows each member to see his or her value and place in the family.

Materials: 1 paper-covered "bottle" (with wide rim) per person, pens/markers, colorful paper, and/or magazines for collages.

Description: Each of you will design your own bottle to describe yourself. You then exchange written appreciation notes with other members of your family.

Directions:

- Give each person a bottle and instruct him or her to decorate it in a way that describes themselves, writing their names, and including hobbies, favorites, personality traits, meaningful objects, etc.
- After finishing the bottles, each member explains the significance of different pictures or words on his/her bottle.
- Distribute small pieces of paper and ask each family member to write a note for each person in the family, saying what they appreciate about that person, and depositing the notes in the respective bottles.
- Each person should end up with messages from every other person in the family.

*Younger children may need to draw and explain verbally what their drawing mean.

How can we appreciate our differences?

Understanding each other is a key to being able to offer love and acceptance. Just as each person has different strengths, there are differences in needs, means of showing and receiving love, and ways of coping when facing change. Some people need more hugs than others, some need to hear encouraging words. While some people are very outgoing, others do better when getting some time alone. Instead of assuming that everyone else thinks the same way, learning to see from the perspective of others can help your family work well together. As parents, you also show your best leadership when working together to use your differences in ways that complement each other and help each other grow. The more your family appreciates each other, the better you work together and support one another.

Points to Ponder:

Now is a good opportunity to create a deeper sense of understanding of each other and to start a pattern of encouraging each other.

- What makes each of you unique?

_____

_____

_____

_____

_____

Everybody is different in how much they like to be around others, how they perceive others, how they make decisions, and how organized or flexible they are. These differences are normal; there is no "right" or "wrong" personality.[6]

- What differences do you notice about each other? Who is the most outgoing? Who needs personal time? Are some more logical? Others more aware of emotions? Who likes structure? How about being spontaneous?

_____

_____

_____

_____

_____

_____

_____

[6] One description of these differences comes with the Myers-Briggs Personality types, also described in "Please Understand Me 2" by David Keirsey.

_____

_____

_____

_____

_____

Each person is also different in how they show love to others
and what makes them feel loved. There are five common ones[7]:

     1) Encouraging words

     2) Acts of service

     3) Gifts

     4) Touch

     5) Quality time together

Talking about this makes it easier to be aware of when someone else trying to show love,
and know the best way to make others feel loved.

- What makes each of you feel loved? How do you show love to each other? Brainstorm
  specific ways to show love to each family member.

_____

_____

_____

_____

_____

_____

_____

_____

_____

_____

_____

_____

---

[7] For more detail you can read "The Five Love Languages" by Gary Chapman.

20

Part 2: Cooperation, Connection, and Communication

How does our crew function?

"Be completely humble and gentle; be patient, bearing with one another in love. Make every effort to keep unity of the Spirit through the bond of peace."   Ephesians 4:2-3

How do we work together?

In order for any ship to set sail, it needs a crew that knows how to communicate well and work together. To do that, each member needs to know where he or she fits in the picture and how to get along with other members. This cooperation works best when following the example of Jesus and his disciples. Each was unique, but they all learned to have servant hearts and act out of love. They grew to understand each other, despite their differences.

In Part 1 you looked at your individual differences, and now we can go a step further to explore what that means for diverse roles you play. On a ship, crew members have different positions, such as the captain, first mate, communications officer, seamen, engineers, and stewards. In the same way, your family can find unique parts for each member to play based on his or her strengths. This approach not only helps meet each others' needs, it shows how important each person is. Your family can feel more like a team and find more ways to encourage each other.

Points to Ponder:

It is important for each member to find a specific role that he/she can play in your family based on each person's identity and strengths. Each person is an integral part of the crew, and there is no one role superior to another.

- Parents, talk to your kids about the illustration of a ship's crew and the need for multiple roles to keep the ship functioning (e.g. not everyone on the ship should be an engineer).

- Think back to "Message in the Bottle" and how each of you are each unique. How does that fit with the illustration of a ship's crew with different roles?

_____

_____

- Brainstorm about possible roles members of your family can play. What would you be interested in doing along the way? For example the creative one might take photos along the journey, the organized one can help pack and count luggage, and the explorer can find out more about the culture where the family is headed.

_____

_____

_____

_____

_____

_____

_____

_____

- Working as a team often includes helping cover each other's duties when they are not available. In different or unexpected situations new roles often appear. How do you notice when someone needs help? What are good ways to ask for help?

_____

_____

_____

_____

_____

_____

_____

_____

Who leads the crew?

Good leadership is critical for a crew to function well. As parents, you hold that responsibility, making it critical that you have a cooperative system of leadership. That includes appreciating and making use of each others' strengths in a mutually supportive relationship. When both of you take an active role in nurturing, sheltering, and directing your children, you provide a greater sense of security for them.

In the brand new culture, your children will need to sense both protection and permission to take appropriate "risks." These risks might be expressing their feelings, riding a bike, or making friends across cultural barriers. Research shows nurturing is not only the mother's role. The father plays a critical part in showing love for the mother and investing in the lives of the children; acceptance or rejection from him has a more powerful effect on the children.[8]

As discussed in Part 1, consistency helps provide security, even though some flexibility is needed at times. This pattern is also true for setting clear guidelines in a way that your children know the standards will be reinforced. It also helps when children understand why rules are in place (e.g. for their safety). This process is not only telling children what they should not do, but also affirming them when they do the right thing. Encouraging words feel good to everyone and should be heard more than criticism and correction. On a long-term basis encouragement is a more effective source of motivation. As parents, you should also be aware that you are constantly acting as role models. Holding yourselves to the same standards sets an example for your children to follow.

Points for Parents to Ponder:

It is important for you as parents to take time to think about what your parenting goals and priorities are. This dialog helps develop a cooperative system of leadership. Coming to agreements ahead of time prevents being in conflict in front of your children.

---

[8] Wickstrom, D. (1998). *The importance of fathers in MK development.* Morris, D. (1998). *Raising resilient MKs.*

- Take time individually and write on separate pieces of paper your top three strengths in the role as a family leader and the top three challenges in your partnership.
- Get back together and read your responses to each other. Take turns sharing, listening, and then responding.
- Write down a couple of the key strengths and weaknesses that you identified:

_____

_____

_____

_____

_____

_____

- Discuss what your priorities as parents are and how they can best be maintained using the strengths and challenges you identified.

_____

_____

_____

_____

_____

_____

_____

- Are there any conflicts you've noticed coming up? If so, take some time to talk about them. Now, try to come to an agreement on how to best support each other in your leadership roles. In the space below, write out a commitment to support each other.

_____

_____

_____

_____

_____

_____

_____

- As written above, consistent discipline is a key responsibility for parents. Think about what you've tried in the past. Which do you do more frequently: correct your children's behavior or affirm them? Do your kids know why consequences are in place? Are you using tools such as time-outs, including time to talk about why something is wrong and what would have been the right thing to do? Do you back each other up when the rules and consequences are being enforced?

- Write down strategies for future discipline.

_____

_____

_____

_____

_____

_____

_____

_____

_____

When do we need to listen?

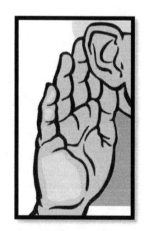

Listening is one of the first skills to learn when looking at communication. As a couple, you must be able to listen to each other for effective leadership. You also need to learn how to listen to the children. Being heard helps someone feel importance and makes it easier for kids to share their thoughts, creating a healthy atmosphere for sharing. Sometimes your children just want someone to listen rather than make immediate judgments or present solutions. Asking questions can help them think through some of their own concerns, although needs vary by individual differences and age. Knowing that you have heard them and feeling understood also helps your children to be more open to receiving your comments. As parents you are always setting an example for your children on communication.

Points for Parents to Ponder:

Now is a chance for you as parents to consider the need to express the importance of each child by listening to him/her and trying to understand him/her.

- Think about times when you felt stressed or frustrated and began telling someone else about it. Were you looking for logical explanations or just someone to listen?

_____

_____

_____

- Children also at times need to express their emotions. Even if there is a "solution" from an adult perspective, the child often just needs to feel heard.
- After your child feels understood and then asks for input he or she will be more open to receiving what you as a parent can explain or recommend.
- Through the process of talking with you, your child might come to the same conclusion by him/herself. Asking questions can help guide their thoughts.
- Your own openness to your children can also facilitate good communication. Listening will make it easier for them to be open in the future.
- Here is a list of ways to talk with your children (from *Families on the Move*[9]):

Do:

- Set aside other things
- Respond- make the sort of noises that show you understand
- Comfort- take it seriously
- Watch your face- don't look horrified even if you feel it
- Inform them of the real state of affairs, especially if they are fearful
- Watch their behavior, their non-verbal communication
- Be positive about the situation
- Check the other side's story before acting

Don't:

- Laugh at them or their fears
- Ignore what they're trying to tell you
- Over-react to what you're told
- Criticize their feelings
- Interrupt them
- Compare them to their siblings
- Say "I'm too busy."
- Embarrass them in front of others

---

[9] Knell, M. (2001). *Families on the move: Growing up overseas and loving it!* London: Monarch Books.

Which of these are you good at doing? Are there any that could use some improvement?

_____

_____

_____

_____

_____

_____

_____

How does the whole family learn to communicate?

Good communication is important for any close relationship. It provides a place to be honest about emotions, sharing about both challenges and encouraging moments. Talking is a way to express love to each other. It is a chance for you to include humor to cheer each other up and reduce tension. Starting early in life is the easiest way to make good communication a habit. Thus, helping your children improve their listening skills and providing a place where they can express concerns serves as a solid foundation.

Siblings can also have a profound effect on each others' lives, often positive when exchanging care, friendship and practical help. It is especially important to be able to communicate within your family when entering a new culture, often a new language, where it takes time to learn to communicate there. This makes the current relationship-building very important, while also setting examples for future relationships.

Activity: Pass the Ship's Radio

Objective: To develop open family communication and practice active listening, in a safe setting where all family members are on equal ground.

Materials: One "radio" (you can create one by decorating a juice box or by drawing a picture); optional questions to ask

Description: Your family unit will spend time together, asking questions, sharing thoughts, and listening to each other. Each person has a chance to do each process, and only one person—the one who holds the radio—is allowed to speak at a time.

Directions: When using a ship's radio only one person can talk at a time, or neither person will hear the other. The same principle is used here so that each person can listen and feel heard when speaking. In this activity, find an object to represent a radio. Clarify the main rule: Only the person holding the radio can talk.

- Give the radio to a family member. That first person asks a second person a question, then passes the radio to that person.
- The second person answers and hands the radio to a third person, who restates the second person's answer, then gives the radio back to the second person.
- The second person agrees or clarifies, then asks a new question and passes the radio.
- Talk afterwards about the experience. How did it feel to know someone was listening when they repeated your answer? Was it hard to stay quiet? Did you learn something new about each other?

Parents: You can create a list of questions beforehand that might be good ways to get to know each other and to share openly. One option is to write the questions on slips of paper and have each person draw one and read it when it is his or her turn.

Samples questions:
- Describe someone who has been a good friend and what was special about that person.
- What do you do when you are feeling very sad or depressed?
- Which was the best vacation you've ever had in your life?
- What makes your angry? How do you overcome your anger?
- If you could have lunch with anybody (real or from a story), who would you choose and why?

- Tell your favorite memory of something the family did together.
- What do look forward to the most when thinking about going to a new country?
- If you could to anything for a day, what would you do?
- Which is your favorite time of the day: are you a morning person or a night person?
- What is the craziest thing you have ever done?
- Which is the funniest prank played on you or played by you?
- If given a choice, which animal would you want to be? Why?
- What is your favorite place on this earth?
- If you were stranded on a lonely beach, what are the five items that you would want to have to survive?
- What is your biggest fear about moving?

*Simpler questions may be used for younger children.

How can we deal with conflict?

Hand-in-hand with establishing healthy strategies for communication is the need to address pre-existing sources of conflict in your family. Problems in relationships tend to get worse when adding stress, such as a big transition. Those problems can lead to more mistrust at a time when reliability in your family is critical. Frequent conflict between you, the parents, directly affects your children. It makes it harder to find a sense of security, which is needed for good communication. It doesn't mean there should never be conflict. That is inevitable! What is important is knowing how to deal with it. It requires being honest with each other, practicing those listening skills, and solving the problems that arise. If there are any unsolved problems or barriers, it is best to settle them as soon as possible in order for you to be able to learn well together.

Points to Ponder:

Parents: Now is a good chance to identify barriers present in current relationships (i.e. between parent and child, between siblings) and make an effort to work through them. Here are some steps for you to take:

29

- Talk with your children about the importance of being open to one another; keeping negative emotions inside does not help anyone.

- Ask each child if he/she feels comfortable opening up to other family members when something goes wrong.

- If you notice any barriers between you and one of your children, find some time to talk one-on-one with him or her in a safe context. Use those listening skills.

- If there are problems between siblings, the two should have a chance to express those, with a parent present as a moderator.

- Before any discussion, remind everyone of the importance of listening, and keep the "radio" available if needed to give each one a chance to express how he/she feels.

Activity: Do you know your crew?

Objective: To allow your family members see how much they know about other members.

Materials: Spinning arrow or bottle, cards with simple questions written on them (e.g. What is _____'s favorite color?). Questions from last activity may also be included.

Description: Your family can play this game sitting in a circle with the spinner in the middle, taking turns around the circle. When a person has a turn, he or she spins the arrow and draws a card. The person reads the question, then tries to answer it about the person to whom the arrow is pointing. That person confirms or corrects the answer. Members discover what they know about each other or learn new things.

Directions: Distribute the cards and spinners, and explain the format of the game. Decide beforehand how many rounds you want to have to complete the game and make sure you have enough question cards.

- Each question counts for a certain number of points (as decided by parents), and the player with the highest score from answering questions correctly wins.

- After the game is over have each person share the most interesting thing they learned about another family member.

Sample questions:

- Favorite color
- Favorite book
- Favorite song
- Favorite food

- Favorite movie
- Favorite animal
- Favorite holiday

(If person doesn't have a "favorite" give 2 options: Does _____ like red or blue more?)

- Name 3 toys/hobbies _____ has
- What was _____ doing yesterday afternoon?
- Name one of _____'s friends
- Describe a decoration in _____'s room
- What is _____'s middle name?
- Questions from "Pass the Radio"

Part 3: Developing a Common Perspective

Charting out the course

"And we know that in all things God works for the good of those who love him, who have been called according to his purpose."   Romans 8:28

Are we going the same direction?

In order for a ship to reach its destination, the whole crew should be following the same map. In other words, everyone needs to understand in what direction they are going and what steps need to be taken to steer the ship. The crew should also be aware of the purpose of the journey and be able to keep that purpose as a central focus. Talking through these topics is a great chance to practice communication skills. It is a chance to make sure that your children are "on board" with the decisions being made.

Including your children in decision-making may seem more complicated than simply making all the decisions for your family as parents. However, achieving a family consensus helps your children develop a greater sense of commitment and investment in family goals. This reward is worthwhile for the time and effort invested. It is also a place to practice your communication skills. You still need to maintain your authority in order to provide the secure leadership for a healthy family. At the same time, you can allow children to offer views and preferences that are carefully weighed and considered as part of the process. As children mature and increase in responsibilities, their contributions should hold greater weight in family decisions.

Points for Parents to Ponder:

Parents: Here is a chance for you to make sure that you are both on the same track, and then share your plans and goals with your children.

- Start by spend time together, thinking about these questions:
- What is your overall purpose for going overseas, practically and spiritually?

_____

_____

_____

- What are your short-term goals as you prepare for departure?

_____

_____

_____

_____

- What steps are you planning to take to move towards those goals?

_____

_____

_____

_____

- Now you have a chance to share these wider goals and concrete steps with your children. Be ready to answer the "why" questions they might have.
- It is important that they feel they can ask questions and, as a result, have a better understanding of the direction the "ship" is heading.
- As you respond, acknowledge your children's comments and questions as valid, offering what explanations are available, and confirming that your children are an important part of the decision-making process.
- In the space below you can write down some of the questions and ideas for future reference.
- Kids: Do you have ideas you want to share about upcoming plans? Is there anything you are worried about? Do you have any other questions?

_____

_____

_____

_____

_____

_____

_____

_____

_____

Where are we going?

It is also critical that your children be given the chance to voice their own ideas of where the boat is headed. This time to talk also helps ensure that their views are accurate. Communication needs to be clear and genuine in order to avoid confusion and to prevent unneeded worry. For example, a child who is told the family is moving to Africa may think it is a place of dangerous wild beasts, and may thus be afraid about what was ahead. Your kids' anxiety about the impending change can be reduced by giving clear information and encouraging them to feel free to ask questions as they arise. It also helps to keep them involved in the preparation and included in the decision-making.

Activity: What's on the Map?

Objectives: To identify the viewpoints and expectations of each member and see how they compare to the rest of your family. To give children an opportunity to express their current understanding or confusion about what to expect and to clarify misconceptions when necessary.

Materials: Pens/pencils, paper "maps" (make copies of included map)

Description: Each person will "map-out" what changes they think will occur, with one paper for each of the following: Family, friends, community, church, school, location, and language. Your family will then gather and compare notes, parents making clarifications as necessary.

Directions: Let each person have one map for each topic. In the area provided, write or draw how you see things now and what they expect it to be like when going overseas.

- When all members of the family are finished—older children working alone while parents guide the younger ones—you can come together and compare notes.
- Parents gain insight on their children's expectations and perspective, and make clarifications for unrealistic/ inaccurate expectations.
- If a child learns something, he or she can write it on the back of the appropriate map.

Maps included: One with lines for writing, one without lines for drawing.

What is it like now?

_____

_____

_____

_____

_____

_____

_____

_____

CHANGES

What's Next?

_____

_____

_____

_____

_____

_____

_____

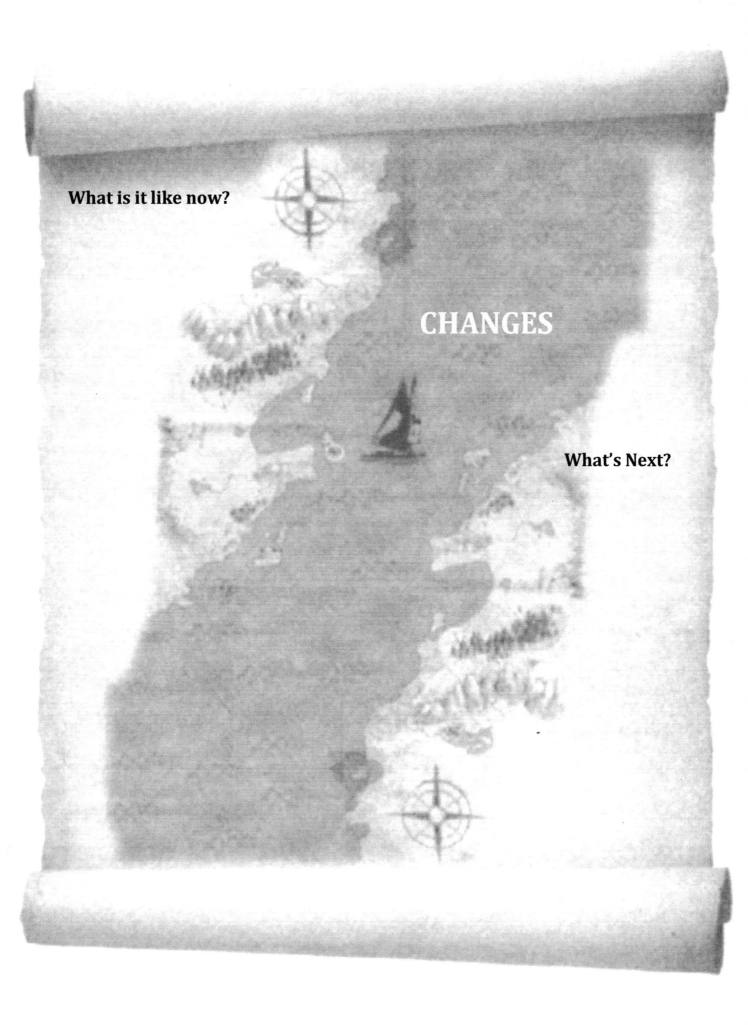

How do we get on the same page?

A system of regular "crew meetings" is a great place to put your learned communication skills to use. It can provide a safe place for expressing feelings and addressing worries. Meeting once a week provides a chance to talk about current or upcoming events. Including your children in the process helps them feel valued as a member of the family. Spending time together also leads to a greater sense of unity. In addition to talking about concerns, your crew meetings can include humor and creativity. This approach fosters a positive environment and an enjoyable process.

Practicing successful crew meetings provides a valuable chance for you to discuss concrete issues that will affect your children's lives. For example, making decisions about education in a new country can be challenging. Even if you have already come to a conclusion, it helps your children, especially older ones, to know why the decision was made and what it means for their lives. The choice between options such as homeschooling, an international school, a local school, and a boarding school affects every aspect of your child's life. It helps kids to know how the decision is in their best interest. Children should gradually take a more active role in making decisions, particularly as adolescents grow in maturity and responsibility.

Activity: Crew Meeting

Objectives: To set a pattern for regular communication times, each member playing an active role and having freedom to be honest. To develop a system for the decision-making process.

Materials: "Ship's log" notebook, "ice breaker" questions

Description: Your family will gather for a "crew meeting," first deciding on the role of each person. The ship's log notebook will be used to keep records of the meetings, and will also be available to any member of the family who would like to write down ideas, questions, and suggestions of issues to be addressed in the next meeting.

Directions: This activity is a chance to show the importance of the different roles. Each person plays an important part in the crew meeting. Start by deciding who will take each role: icebreaker, recorder, discussion leader, and activity planning leader (if applicable). Parents with younger children may play most of these roles, but think creatively of ways they can contribute. For this first meeting, one of the parents should be the discussion leader and can use the following "Points to Ponder."

- The person serving as *icebreaker* reads a written question for the family at the beginning of the meeting (e.g. If you could live one day as a certain animal, which would you choose and why?)

- The *recorder* of the ship's log has the role of writing-down what is discussed and what decisions are made or conclusions are drawn.

- Parents can use the discussion time to address any concerns that came up in the expectation activity or any other issue at hand.

- Each person should have the chance to ask questions, express feelings and offer input.

- After the meeting have a debrief session for family members to share what they liked and disliked about it.

- This meeting can be used on a weekly basis to provide a consistent time for open communication, though not necessarily structured in the exact same way.

- Other fun activities can be included to make it an enjoyable time.

- If needed, the radio can be used to prevent multiple people from attempting to speak at the same time.

-

* Families with younger children may have a simplified discussion and may not need to address as many topics.

Points to Ponder:

Parents: This discussion can be used as the first crew meeting.

Now is a time to develop a common mission statement and to discuss practical issues such as timing, schools, etc.

- Earlier, you as parents talked about some of your short term goals. Spend time brainstorming about goals for the new location (e.g. following God, loving others, being servants, learning about a new culture, etc). Make sure to ask for input from the children.

  _____

  _____

  _____

  _____

  _____

- How would you prioritize these ideas? What is most important to you as a family?

  _____

  _____

  _____

  _____

- Develop a mission statement stating your family purpose and means of reaching those goals (e.g. "Our family's purpose is to love God, love each other, and love others through our words, time, and service.").

  _____

  _____

  _____

  _____

- Talk through issues like education and any other issue brought up in earlier dialogue, and put decisions in the perspective of how they fit-in the family mission statement.

  _____

  _____

_____

_____

_____

_____

_____

_____

_____

Who is sending us?

If your family is being sent overseas by an organization or church, knowing more about who is sending them will help your children to feel more involved in the process. You should also be aware that your own interaction with the organization shapes your children's views. If they hear you express frustration about people or policies, your kids are likely to have a more negative perspective. In contrast, you can emphasize the value of partnership. This approach sets an example of how to work with others. It is also helpful for your children to understand what your roles in the new setting will be. Your kids should be able to answer basic questions about your work, in a way that is appropriate to the setting, particularly if you are transitioning into a sensitive country. The communication practiced here can provide a foundation for clarity in short-term preparations and expectations for the future.

Points to Ponder:

This discussion is an opportunity to help children better understand the parents' sending organization and upcoming roles. Parents can talk through this topic with the children:

- What are the key reasons for partnering with this organization? What roles do the parents and family have working with them?

_____

_____

_____

_____

- Some questions frequently come up both in the home country and overseas. What is the best way to answer questions such as, "What do your parents do?" and "Why are you going there?"

_____

_____

_____

_____

_____

- How do these roles and reasons for going match with the family mission statement? How do they fit with the short-term preparations? The long-term outcome?

_____

_____

_____

_____

_____

- Any other questions?

_____

_____

_____

_____

_____

_____

_____

_____

_____

_____

_____

_____

Part 4: Preparing for Departure

Get ready to lift the anchor

"While they were worshiping the Lord and fasting, the Holy Spirit said, 'Set apart for me Barnabas and Saul for the work to which I have called them.' So after they had fasted and prayed, they placed their hands on them and sent them off."
                                                                    Acts 13: 2-3

How do we get ready to leave?

For a ship to have a smooth departure, the crew must know what steps to take and how to do so. It is also important to keep in mind the primary reason for departure: God's calling. It can be comforting to know that God is present wherever your family goes. But it does not mean the process is easy or natural. Specific steps are still needed to get ready. A critical part of the process of leaving is creating a healthy sense of closure, recognizing losses, and allowing time to grieve. Seeking closure is similar to making sure the moorings are released before the ship attempts to leave the harbor.

In the process of letting go, you must be aware of your children's needs, including the ones they cannot describe. Part of your job is to facilitate healthy closure and ways to process the changes at hand. You can start by making sure all members of the family have a clear understanding that emotional reactions are normal and acceptable. When someone tries to bury those emotions, it can later contribute to bitterness or depression. As discussed earlier, your family needs to be a safe place where members can express their feelings to whatever extent they feel the need. In response, your family can offer each other support and affirmation.

It is also important to recognize that individuals have different means of working through the changes at hand. Everyone is unique and should not be expected to respond in the same way to similar circumstances. Some need to have someone listening as they vent emotions. Others need time alone to think through all that is happening. Each person needs a different amount of time to reach a sense of closure. Parents often have begun the process much earlier than their kids, and should be aware that the kids have had less time to accept the upcoming changes.

Points to Ponder:

Here is a chance to talk about the process of goodbyes and grieving (and that it's okay to do so), and to emphasize the importance of support and affirmation.

- Think about a time when something sad happened and how you reacted.
- Feeling sad when having to say goodbyes is normal, and each person does it in a different way. Share with your family how you react to hard experiences.
- Don't forget that it is actually good to allow emotions to come out instead of letting them bottle up inside you. How comfortable so you feel sharing your emotions?
- Think about what is comforting for you during a tough time. What support would be helpful during that time? Record ways each person would feel supported when sad or lonely (e.g. a hug, a reminder that it is okay to express themselves, etc.)

_____

_____

_____

_____

_____

_____

_____

_____

_____

- Going through many changes and saying goodbyes can be overwhelming, and it takes time to fully understand and accept all that is happening.
- The ways individuals are unique also affects how they process all that is going on around them. Some do their processing more by thinking logically, some focus more on their feelings. While some find it helpful to process through talking with someone else, others need more time alone to think through it.

- After talking about the differences between members of your family, how do you think all that you have learned about yourselves and each other is applicable here?

_____

_____

_____

_____

- This is another great chance to make an effort to understand other family members, and to help others understand you.
- It can be helpful at times to vent emotions to others who are willing to just listen, to process internally, to ask questions, to journal, to draw pictures to illustrate their feelings, or other means of expression.
- There are times when a family member needs someone to be there to comfort them in the present. Other times it can be helpful to look toward the future, offering encouragement about what lies ahead.

What does it mean to leave things behind?

Leaving includes grieving the loss of whatever is left behind. A big part of this is the special people in each of your lives, whether grandparents, teachers, friends, neighbors, or anyone important to each family member. Pets are often very special to a family, and saying goodbye to them is often difficult. Not everyone thinks about also saying goodbye to places that hold special memories and meaningful objects that don't all fit in the boxes. Everyone is different, and it may not be as intense for some of you as it will be for others. It is still important to make sure there is space for feelings, with no need to hide sadness.

One woman who grew up overseas realized later that not dealing with hidden grief had negative effects all the way into adulthood. She expressed that unresolved grief is one of the most significant burdens of the mobile lifestyle.[10] She wrote, "Grief happens and it can't be reasoned with. The truth is there's only one way out of it - and that is by going through it." There are often intangible or "hidden" losses that can easily be overlooked. Not

---

[10] Carlson, D. (1997). *Being a global nomad: The pros and cons*. Publications web site: http://www.worldweave.com/procon.htm

only are special objects and important people left behind, but a familiar role is gone, and a sense of status disappears. For some, an entire lifestyle is lost, including the potential experiences it might have included. Recognizing and allowing time to grieve for these losses contributes to healthy closure.

Activity: What Stays on the Dock

Objective: To give children a chance to process what they will be leaving behind and identify where closure is needed.

Materials: Paper (two sheets per person), markers or crayons

Descriptions: Here your children will be given a chance to express what they want to leave behind and what they know they will miss.

Directions: Distribute paper and talk briefly about the things that they will not be able to bring on the ship with them, instead leaving them on the dock, including people, places, possessions and pets.

- On one paper each one of you can list or draw pictures of what is special to you that you will have to leave behind.
- Using a different colored marker or crayon on the second paper, make a list or draw pictures of what you are glad you will be leaving behind.
- Talk together as a family about what was written or drawn. As parents, you can share a couple of examples, and then let each child share one or two things from each list, and why they are on the list.
- Brainstorm good ways to say goodbye, such as visiting special places, taking picture with people who are important to them, etc.

_____

_____

_____

_____

How do we know when we're ready to go?

Getting ready to say goodbyes to the people and things that are important to you is just one component of the departure process. One tool developed for facilitating healthy grieving in the midst of transition is the RAFT, which was developed by David Pollock:[11]

Older Children	Younger Children
Reconciling conflict with others	**R**emember to make things **R**ight with others
Affirming the relationships you have had	**A**lways being thankful for good friends
Farewell to people, places, pets, possessions	**F**arewell to what was special
Thinking ahead by gathering information about your new host countries	**T**hinking about what's next

Pollock emphasizes the importance of resolving conflicts before leaving instead of ignoring them. Children can be asked if there is anyone they need to ask for forgiveness or anyone they have not forgiven. These questions can lead to taking steps toward reconciliation. It is also important to look at the positive friendships you have and to think of practical ways to keep in touch. It takes a conscious effort to facilitate needed goodbyes. Your family can apply these concepts with tangible activities such as making a memory book or visiting a favorite place, which can create positive memories.

At the same time, your family can also look practically and realistically towards the destination. Upcoming challenges must be recognized so they can be addressed. These might include the loss of having an established role, knowing where you fit in to society. Having people around you who know you helps you feel comfortable with who you are. When losing that part of your identity, it can feel difficult to start from scratch.

Communication skills and mutual support between family members are again crucial during this period of uprooting. Your family is one of the few constants in the midst of a many losses and changes. Family members can help each other work toward the balance between keeping a positive outlook but the feeling accepted when needing to express emotions.

---

[11] Pollock, D., & Van Reken, R. (2009). *Third culture kids: Growing up among worlds*. London: Nicholas Brealy Publishing.

Activity: Building the RAFT

Objective: To help the family work through aspects of closure together, children expressing what is important to them, and parents providing a larger context.

Materials: Popsicle sticks, glue, markers, ship's log

Description: Your family has already gone through the process of identifying what you will leave behind. That can be used as a stepping stone toward making a symbolic raft and explaining the four aspects of closure. You will create practical ideas of activities you can do as family to help bring closure.

Directions: Take the popsicle sticks and build a raft, dividing it into four sections. You can do one for the whole family, or have each individual make and decorate one.

- On each section write one aspect of closure, and explain each one to your children.
- Refer back to the previous activity, when members identified the relationships that they would be glad to end. Are any of those relationships that might need reconciliation?
- Talk about the most important relationships, how to affirm and show love to those individuals, and practical ways to stay in touch.
- As a family, think back to the ideas gathered when you brainstormed about ways to say goodbye. Come up with practical activities to help the process, and record them in the ship's log.
- Spend some time talking about upcoming practical steps in the moving process.

What will this look like in the future?

The act of leaving begins a new way of life that will shape each family member's identity. The effects are evident particularly in children who spend many years overseas. Children who grow up in a culture distinct from their parent's home culture are often known as "third culture kids" (TCKs) or "global nomads." The term "third culture" means that children do not feel fully part of their parents' culture (1st), or the host culture or cultures (2nd) where they live. Instead they share a "third culture" with others who have

had similar life experiences of high mobility and a cross-cultural childhood. The positive and negative dynamics of this way of life will be addressed in a later section. However, it will help you as parents to be aware from the start that their children are developing a perspective different from your own "home" culture. You can make an effort to ensure that this new viewpoint enriches your children's lives.

Points for Parents to Ponder:

You may have already heard of third culture kids, but it helps to make an effort to be aware of what that means in your family.

- As parents, you are representatives of the first culture in your children's lives. Depending on where you live, they will have a variety of other sources of exposure to your home culture (e.g. media, other foreigners, and long-distance contact with friends). What are trends in your culture that your children might experience within your home? (e.g. norms for meals, traditions, etc.)

_____

_____

_____

_____

- What are some components of your home culture that they won't see or experience directly? Think of things that you experienced growing up that they will not (e.g. school system, direct exposure to fashion trends, music, etc.).

_____

_____

_____

_____

- Your children will combine the trends and norms they see from you with what they experience in the surrounding cultures. This combination gives them a different perspective, one that can be positive and insightful in many ways. Their cross-cultural experience also shapes their entire identity as they relate to other individuals with a similar lifestyle rather than remaining part of only one culture.

- As you prepare to leave, it is important that you also seek closure in the awareness that the geographic place you are leaving will never be the same "home" to your children as it was to you. Mixed feelings are normal, as is the process of grieving. What might be difficult for you to leave behind?

_____

_____

_____

_____

- At the same time, much of the leaving process can be seen in a positive light when finding support from family and friends and taking the upcoming voyage as a privilege, an opportunity to serve God and widen your perspective. What can you do to keep that in mind and to encourage each other?

_____

_____

_____

_____

_____

Part 5: Coping with Stress and Conflicts

Dealing with stormy weather

"We are hard pressed on every side, but not crushed; perplexed, but not in despair; persecuted, but not abandoned; struck down, but not destroyed."
Acts 13: 2-3

How do we face stress?

Some journeys are more "stormy" than others, and a crew needs to know how to respond to bad weather in order to prevent severe damage to the ship. It is crucial for each member of your crew to be not only well-prepared but also united with other members. The team can share a clear focus on God, the ultimate Captain, in order to effectively weather a storm. The emotions that come with being away from home add to significant relational tension. Being in the "limbo" state of transition can also be challenging and increase stress. It is helpful for you to have an awareness of these sources of tension and an ability to recognize

conflict at an early stage. Doing so can prevent the distress caused by disagreements from escalating. Without addressing the problems early on, small problems can be blown out of proportion.

Points to Ponder:

Now is a chance to identify the challenges that might arise and to understand the emotional reactions of separation and transition.

- All major changes include challenges, ranging from minor stressors to major crises, just as a ship will hit anything from rough waters to hurricanes.
- Such challenges may be on a practical level (e.g. trouble getting the right documents in order) or on a relational basis (arguments over upcoming plans), particularly with the added stress of uncertainty while in transition.

- What is an example of a challenge you recently faced, or are currently facing?

_____

_____

_____

_____

_____

- It is very important to be aware of the extra tension that comes with times of big transitions and to be able to recognize conflict early on, in order to prevent more damage to a relationship. Think of a time when someone got frustrated or mad. What triggered it? What were the reactions? How was it resolved?

_____

_____

_____

_____

_____

- Negative emotions, such as feeling angry, sad, or overwhelmed, are normal; however, they need to be recognized and processed rather than taken-out on others. Have each person describe a recent negative feeling. What did you say or do when you felt that way? What helped you to feel better, or what would have helped you to feel better?

_____

_____

_____

_____

_____

- It is also important to be aware of how much stress you are dealing with so you can understand your reactions and know when you need to take a break. See Appendix C for assessing vulnerability to stress.

How do we deal with negative reactions?

How you view a situation or challenge results in an emotional reaction. Your emotions affect your response, which then influences the challenge itself. This pattern becomes cyclical: situation → emotions → response →situation. In such a pattern, a negative event or conversation can cause your family members to feel angry or overwhelmed. Those feelings make it more difficult to find solutions, making the problem look even bigger that it is.

Activity: Drop the Anchor

Objective: To help your family identify sources of anger and typical responses through coping strategies, and learn effective ways to deal with negative reactions with basic tools and methods for problem solving.

Materials: An anchor for the family, cardboard, glue, pens, pencils, or crayons

Description: Each member of your family will share about a time when he/she got angry and how he/she responded. Reactions will be discussed and conflict management tools introduced.

Directions: Ask each person to share with the family about an event that made him/her feel angry. Why did you feel that way? What you do in response?

- There are two common negative responses: withdrawing or lashing back. Those reactions will not help to solve the problem. If you withdraw, it is like burying the anger, which often lets it grow and sprout up again later. Lashing back usually makes the other person feel angry or hurt, which can cause the same reactions. But there is another good way to respond.
- It is very important to listen to the other person's side of the story, make an effort to have empathy (think about how they feel), and honestly share your own feelings. Then you can work together to find a resolution and to decide what each person needs to do to improve the situation.

56

- Picture being on a ship in a storm. What would happen if you ignore the storm? What about if you get frustrated at the storm? Neither will help stabilize the boat. Instead one needs to drop the anchor, and when the boat is stabilized check for damage and make repairs.

- In the same way if conflict levels are escalating, it is often most effective to step back and take time to cool down. Then try again to address the real problem, not the emotions coming out of it.

- Make a copy of the anchor and glue it on a piece of cardboard, decorating it however you like as a family.

- Plan what to do the next time a conflict arises, and write something brief on the anchor as a reminder. A statement such as "I need to drop the anchor," can be used to signify the need to step back and cool down.

How can we settle conflicts?

Everyone is unique, and with that often comes differences of opinion. Those differences can also lead to disagreements among the members of your family, but disagreements are not necessarily harmful. Some disagreements can be on much more

touchy subjects than others. There are three common responses to an argument: avoid the issue at hand, act or speak in an unkind or angry way, or work together to find a resolution. Conflict in your family can be hurtful. But it can also be a chance to practice problem-solving. Working together can actually lead to greater unity and deeper intimacy, even when started by an argument.

Already we have put a lot of focus on building good communication patterns and understanding each other. The same principles apply here, with more specific methods for problem-solving and coping strategies. Key skills are learning to take another person's perspective, controlling reactions, and resolving disagreements.

To effectively deal with a problem, your family must first acknowledge it. As parents, you can help guide a discussion, making sure everyone feels included and valued. Together, your family can brainstorm for solutions. Harmful conflict comes when each person focuses on winning the argument. In order to replace the conflict with cooperation, each of you needs to be sensitive toward the other person and keep an open mind. Using criticism, blame, or avoidance of the problem never helps. Instead, the focus should be on a common goal, based on what is best for your whole family.

Thus, the first step is to agree on a realistic goal. Then, your family can think of specific steps to take toward that goal. After taking those steps it helps to look at the situation again. If positive change has come from it, it is encouraging to see those results of working together. Reviewing what happened can also help see what mistakes might have been made in order to avoid making them again. It is important to avoid blaming each other; instead focus on positive steps to take in the future.

Points to Ponder:

Now is a time for your family to talk about ways to address conflict. You can guide the discussion, telling your children about ways to find resolutions.

- Disagreements are normal and inevitable because everyone is different. The question is how do we respond? The 3 common responses are: 1) avoiding the problem; 2) respond in a negative way, such as anger or hurtful words; or 3) making an attempt to cooperate.

- What do you do when in a conflict? What do you notice about others in the family?

_____

_____

_____

_____

- Each of the responses to disagreements leads to a different outcome. What do you think happens when you avoid talking about a problem? What about when you get angry?

_____

_____

_____

_____

- These first two reactions can easily lead to misunderstanding and hurt feelings. If not addressed, it may eventually turn into a damaged relationship. This sad outcome is another example of the importance of clear communication.

- Choosing the third response, looking for ways to work together find a resolution, can result in a deeper intimacy and stronger relationships. Can you think of a time when you were able to solve a disagreement? How did it feel to have it behind you?

_____

_____

_____

_____

- It can help to have specific steps to take when dealing with conflict. Here is one way to deal with a problem:
  1. The family must acknowledge its presence.
  2. Open communication is needed, with each member able to share freely, as mediated by the parents.
  3. Replace hostility and competition with mutual sensitivity and open-mindedness, making an effort to see the other person's view rather than resorting to criticism, blame, or avoidance.
  4. Focus on common goals that would be best for both parties and the family as a whole.
  5. Outline specific steps that can be taken toward the goal.
  6. After a set period of time assess the issue, considering whether the agreed upon steps have been taken, whether they are effective, and what needs to be changed or added.
- Think of a recent disagreement. What would it look like to follow these steps as a family?

_____

_____

_____

_____

_____

_____

_____

_____

- At first it can be a big challenge to go through the whole process of problem-solving. But if used regularly, it can eventually become a pattern and can overall contribute to healthy family relationships.

Activity: Building Bridges

Objective: To work cooperatively to build a bridge, deal with frustration, and solve problems, while emphasizing the importance of mutual support in stressful circumstances.

Materials: A timer, 2 large containers of water, 2 sets of building materials such as popsicle sticks, paper clips, string, tape, and similar small items available. Keeping the items small and simple makes the activity more challenging.

Description: Your family will work together to build a bridge, but each family member is allowed to only use one hand when building. The need for cooperation will be shown when bridges are made with and without the ability to talk.

Directions: Bridges are an important way to get across water or other obstacles. It is important for bridges to be well-built; otherwise those who cross may fall through.

- Create to 2 similar sets of building materials and set-up a large container of water for each.
- Every family member is only allowed to use one hand. During the first attempt, no one is allowed to speak.
- Set the timer for 15 minutes, and during that time work together to build a bridge from one side of the container to the other.
- How did it feel to not be able to speak to each other?

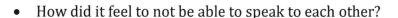

_____

_____

_____

_____

- Complete the challenge again, this time allowing only 7 minutes. Each person still only uses one hand, but now everyone is allowed to talk to each other.

- Compare the two bridges. Which is stronger? Which was easier to construct?

_____

_____

_____

- Talk about the process of building the bridge. What did you do to work together? How did you handle any frustrations or conflict that came up?

_____

_____

_____

_____

_____

- Take a photo of the two bridges to remember the results of your teamwork and good communication.

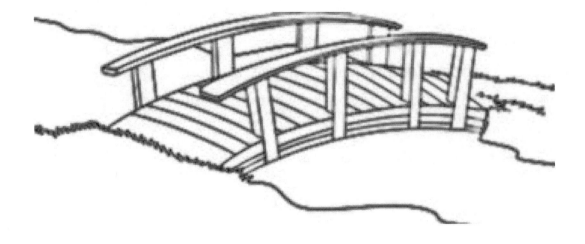

Part 6: Cross-Cultural Transition

Sailing in unfamiliar territory and docking in a new port

"Consequently, you are no longer foreigners and aliens, but fellow citizens with God's people and members of God's household, built on the firm foundation of the apostles and prophets, with Christ Jesus himself as the chief cornerstone... And in him you too are being built together to become a dwelling in which God lives by his Spirit." Ephesians 2: 19-20, 22

How can we be flexible and consistent?

Regardless of how old someone is, entering a new culture can feel like starting a new life. You must learn how to communicate all over again, and how to work with others in a brand new place. Change is inevitable, so your family has to learn ways to be flexible. The overall ability to adapt is a good predictor of how well a family or relationship will thrive. When every part of life is shifting, being able to adapt is especially critical to starting life new in a new place.

In the midst of adjustment, it helps to have some areas of stability. Stability can come by keeping what your family has decided is critical to your identity. This includes values, traditions, sacred objects and memories. Holding on to rituals and routines can help maintain a sense of continuity between what was left behind and what is ahead. Keeping what is important for your family identity also reinforces family ties in the midst of change. Your family needs to have structure without becoming rigid, and should maintain flexibility, but not chaos.

Points to Ponder:

This discussion is a chance to think about ways to both stay flexible and maintain stability.

- Coming into a new culture is similar to beginning a new life, with differences both in the very basics of daily life and gradually learning all the norms and traditions. What might be different compared to your life right now?

- It is very important to be ready to make changes when entering a new context. What changes might be easiest? What might be the more difficult?

- There is always a need for balance: flexibility is important, but not to the point where there is nothing stable, which can feel like chaos. On the other hand, structure is important, as long as it does not become rigid.
- Stability can be maintained in several areas:
  - Relationships: Maintain communication with friends and family members
  - Standards and Values: While some adaptation may be necessary, parents should uphold most family rules and forms of discipline; this is key to providing a stable environment for children.
  - Rituals and Routines: Having similar patterns can be comforting in a new place, such as bedtime stories or household responsibilities.
  - Traditions: Entering a new culture will include encountering new events and traditions, but some elements from the parents' culture should be observed to provide continuity.
  - Sacred Objects: Each child should be allowed to keep at least one item that he/she holds as meaningful, regardless of location. Having a special toy or stuffed animal beside him/her can make a new place feel like home. There may be certain objects the whole family finds significant, such as decorations that make a new house feel familiar.

- o Memories: Photos can be especially helpful to hold on to memories of people, places, and special events.
- How do the items listed above fit with the family identity discussion in Part 1?

_____

_____

_____

_____

- Your family can also look forward to a new location as a place for discovery and adventure, as long as you go in with openness to new ideas. What are some things you would like to discover about a new culture?

_____

_____

_____

_____

_____

_____

- It always takes effort to reach across cultural barriers, but the long-term outcome is a rich cross-cultural experience. What might be some benefits of being in another culture?

_____

_____

_____

_____

_____

_____

How do we move through the process of transition?

David Pollock and Ruth Van Reken[12] outlined the cross-cultural transition process in five stages. The first, "*Involved*," or feeling settled, is the starting point. It means feeling at home, being involved in the surrounding community, and having a firm understanding of cultural norms. Next comes "*Leaving*," as discussed in Part 4. After that is the "*Transition*" phase, which can be difficult as a sense of normalcy is lost. Sometimes small problems look much bigger than they really are. Self-esteem often plunges when someone feel isolated, having just left his or her own culture and not knowing much about the new culture. Being in a family can help reduce feelings of being alone.

As your family prepares to go into the new culture, you also move into the stage of "*Entering.*" This step only begins when you choose to start the process of engaging with the new culture. It includes a wide range of emotions in the midst of searching for a new role to play. Some of you may feel that you have lost your belongings or the status you had gained in your last home. Others have painful emotions stem from the ongoing grieving process, after saying goodbye to friends, family, and an overall lifestyle. Individual members may feel anxiety from new demands or expectations. Some find a new awareness about their own misconceptions and biases. Once again, mutual support is critical, including the permission to express feelings. It helps to know these feelings are normal and acceptable.

Points to Ponder:

It is to important talk about ways to offer mutual support, including the permission to express emotions. That freedom keeps sharing from feeling uncomfortable, unusual or unacceptable.

- It is normal to go through a process of grieving when leaving home and entering a new place. Often many different emotions emerge in the process, especially when saying a lot of goodbyes.
- Let each person share possible concerns (e.g. being alone, not knowing anyone, anxiety over dealing in a foreign culture, inability to communicate, etc.).

---

[12] Pollock & Van Reken, 2009

_____

_____

_____

_____

_____

_____

- It is important to express your feelings, as you have just done, rather than bottle them up inside. Have you ever had times when you didn't feel it was okay to talk about something?

_____

_____

_____

_____

_____

- What are some ways you can be good listeners and show support for each other?

_____

_____

_____

_____

_____

What does it look like to enter a new culture?

When a crew enters new waters, one of the biggest challenges is learning to effectively communicate with those at the new dock. Many questions of uncertainty exist: Where and how should the ship dock? How can communication links be made to forge crucial relationships? Making friends is a key way to find help getting used to the culture. How can you again earn respect for your life experience, when suddenly feeling ignorant? From the moment your family arrives there will be a need to learn the new norms of daily living. Over time, you learn what is and is not acceptable, as well as more subtle parts of the culture.

It is important to remember the positive aspects of discovery and adventure. Your family has a chance to experience a new culture! Understanding what "culture" means can help you figure out what to look for and what differences to expect. Making a conscious effort to create positive memories in a new setting can help the long-term process of turning the new location into "home." Exploring the new setting and culture as a family can also help reduce anxiety. It can be hard to lose what is "normal" or expected. Communication is more challenging with a language barrier and relationships in the new setting have yet to be developed. It is important to maintain optimism even when change is difficult. Creating a way to encourage each other within your family and using humor can make a difference. These efforts, combined with focusing on what is ahead, eases the tension and increases confidence.

Activity: At a New Port

Objective: To help your family experience cross-cultural interactions and learn how to respond when facing communication challenges and ignorance of cultural norms.

Material: Dinner from another culture served in an unfamiliar context

Description: A dinner will be spent with hosts from a different culture. Family members will not know the language being spoken or the appropriate ways to act or respond. During the whole meal they will attempt to communicate and experience the challenges involved with language barriers.

Directions for Parents: Look for someone in your community from a different culture who is fluent in another language. Ask if they would be willing to host your family for dinner, explaining that you are learning how to relate to other cultures. It may be culturally appropriate to invite them to later come to eat at your house.
* If you have trouble finding someone willing to do this, consult with your church or sending organization, asking if they know someone who would role-play. If there are still no available options, look for a restaurant that caters to another culture.

- Ask your hosts to pretend they cannot understand English, and speak only in a different language. To communicate your family must use other means (hand gestures, trying to learn words, etc.)

- Explain to your hosts that you want to experience their cultural norms. Let them know it is appropriate for them to act offended if you make mistakes, which you can discuss later.

- As a family, think about ways to notice what they do differently and follow their example.

- When dinner is over, ask for feedback on the differences they noticed, mistakes you made, and ways you were able to adapt.

- At home after the experience talk about the following questions as a family:

  o How did it feel to not know what was being said?

  _____

  _____

  _____

  o What was your reaction when you saw that you had offended someone but didn't know how?

  _____

  _____

  _____

  o What was the hardest part about the experience? Why?

  _____

  _____

  _____

  o Is there anything you would have done differently?

  _____

  _____

  _____

o   Is there anything that would have made it easier?

_____

_____

_____

o   Would it have been different if you had been there without other family members? How?

_____

_____

_____

o   What did you learn from the situation?

_____

_____

_____

o   Do you think it would be easier to have the same dinner again, now that you have experience within a different culture?

_____

_____

_____

How do we enter a new culture?

Families need to keep some realistic expectations about cultural transition. There are some big challenges, such as a brand new language. At the same time, you will benefit by creatively exploring chances to expand their experience in their new environment. Jumping right into the new culture is particularly helpful for your children. It allows them to watch, listen, experience, and learn with you, their parents. This exposure helps your children to gain a better picture of the overall culture and to learn how to effectively relate to those around them.

Moving toward "fitting in" comes with learning the basic unwritten rules, attitudes, and traditions of the new culture. This discovery goes hand-in-hand with learning the language, especially when talking directly to locals. Children often find this easier than you, their parents, as learning is always part of a kid's life. It can also help to find a mentor, such as another expatriate who has spent more time in that culture. A good mentor is aware of the differences, knows what it is like to go through change, and is willing to provide support and explanations.

Points to Ponder:

Think about the process of learning a new language and culture as an exciting adventure. It is a chance to experience something new.

- What are possible aspects of cultures that could differ from one country to another (e.g. food, beliefs, etc)?

_____

_____

_____

- Brainstorm possible activities to experience those differences, such as a family trip to the marketplace, or challenging each person to taste a food never eaten before.

_____

_____

_____

- Discuss what you would like/dislike about such experiences, then rank the top three as ones you would try soon after arrival.

_____

_____

_____

- Don't forget it is a learning process, and mistakes are inevitable, as you might have experienced during your cross-cultural dinner experience. It helps to keep a good sense of humor and to encourage each other each step of the way.
- What are the challenges of not knowing the language? What is most daunting for each person?

_____

_____

_____

- How can language-learning be part of the process of experiencing the culture? Do you think it might help to make friends who could be willing to help you learn the language without being overly critical?

_____

_____

_____

_____

- Personality differences can play a big role in how comfortable you are when stepping into a new setting and making new friends. Remember that it is not a contest. Don't put too much pressure on each other. What are ways you can encourage each other and support positive attitudes?

_____

_____

_____

_____

- It may be challenging at times, but remember that the long-term outcome is a valuable expanded worldview!

Where does transition end?

The course of adjustment eventually leads to Pollock's final stage of transition, "*Re-involved*," or feeling settled once again. Gradually, your family takes steps towards once again becoming part of the surrounding community. It takes time to redevelop a sense of security and belonging. Going through the process as a family provides a more constant source of support, as each individual has a chance expand his or her knowledge and experience. Your family also refines its priorities as a result of the challenges faced. While it may seem like a difficult process, out of it comes a stronger sense of responsibility and commitment.

Activity: The Ship's Wheel

Objective: To help the family review and understand the normal transition process and create a visual representation.

Materials: Ship's wheel diagram, cardboard, attachment piece (e.g. a tack), pens, ship's log.

Description: Your family will create a wheel that can be adjusted to have the appropriate stage marked. Stages are described and your family will discuss how to respond at each point.

Directions: A ship's wheel guides the direction of the ship. Turning it takes the ship to different places. In the same way, this wheel represents the process of moving from one stage of transition to the next.

- Cut-out or make a copy of the ship's wheel picture. Attach it to the cardboard at the center, so that it can spin around and draw an arrow at the top of the cardboard, so that it can be adjusted to have the appropriate stage below the arrow.
- Describe how the diagram represents the movement through each stage of transition.
- Review the stages as described through this section, including the normal reactions and emotions at each point.
- Turn the wheel to each stage and take a few minutes to brainstorm how you can support each other during that time.

    o Involved:

    _____

    _____

    _____

    o Leaving:

    _____

    _____

    _____

o   Transition:

_____

_____

_____

o   Entering:

_____

_____

_____

o   Re-involved:

_____

_____

_____

- Which stage might be most difficult? Why?

_____

_____

_____

_____

_____

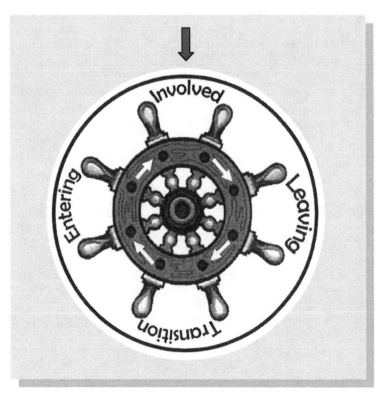

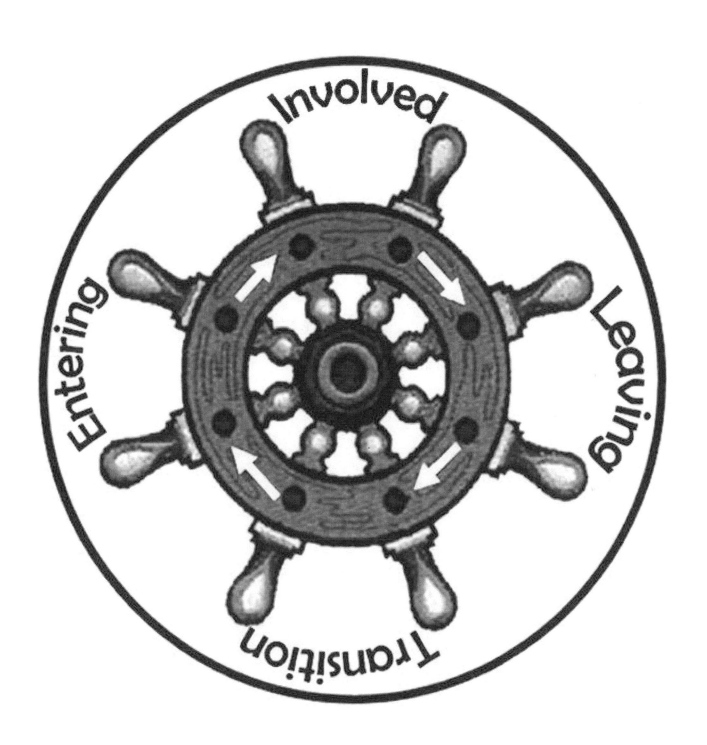

Part 7: The Long-Term Outcome

Ship maintenance and upgrades

"By this all men will know that you are my disciples, if you love one another."

John 13:34-5

Does our family ever change?

As time progresses it is important to keep a ship at its highest functioning capacity. This maintenance includes replacing older materials and parts with newer ones. Often brand new items are added. Even the outward appearance may change as a new layer of paint is applied that is perhaps a different color. In the same way, your family cannot be expected to stay the same. Instead, you can welcome new memories and experiences, which are then integrated into your overall identity. This change does not mean that the original ship will be lost in a complete transformation. If your basic family structure is well-built and resilient, it will remain intact. While the key aspects of your identity are still in place, they may become more complex or you may view them from a different perspective. (See Appendix B for characteristics of a resilient family.)

Points to Ponder:

As you approach the end of this workbook, start thinking about what may come up down the road. There will always be ongoing needs and support systems, and it can help to consider ways of meeting those needs.

- To keep something working well, it needs to be cared for well, and sometimes even upgraded. This reality applies not only to ships, but also to families.
- What have you taken from this program that might be important to keep improving?

_____

_____

_____

_____

- Let each member share a personal need and how it can be met by other family members (e.g. being listened to, receiving encouragement, experiencing fun activities with other family members, etc.).

_____

_____

_____

_____

_____

_____

- What in your family will change as time goes on? (e.g. ages, time spent in the new culture, increase in knowledge and experience, etc.)

_____

_____

_____

_____

_____

_____

- What will, or what do you hope will, stay the same?

_____

_____

_____

_____

_____

_____

- Take time to talk about any further questions or uncertainties about future steps, even if there is no definite answer.

_____

_____

_____

_____

_____

What does it mean to have more than one culture?

When living in another culture it is important to maintain a balance between holding on to your heritage and embracing the host culture. This balance will decrease the sense of uncertainty in your children's developing identity. If you spent most of your life in one culture, you need to be aware that though they share the same nationality, your children are growing up in a new context. As third culture kids (TCKs)—a concept introduced in Part 4—they develop a different cultural perspective from you, their parents. Some TCKs carry their mobile lifestyles into adulthood and now are the parents raising their kids in a similar cross-culture experience. Letting your children know you can relate to them in this experience may be a meaningful way to build relationships.

Being a TCK includes benefits and challenges. One benefit is the ability to be flexible and quickly form deep relationships. But after moving around frequently it can be difficult to put down roots. The many goodbyes to friends may lead to hesitancy to start new relationships. TCKs have multiple cultures built into their identities, producing a broader worldview. At the same time, that view can include exposure to painful realities. Sometimes they feel insecurity about their own culture. (See Appendix A.) It helps TCKs to know that they are not the only ones experiencing these challenges, and that there are other members of this mobile, international third culture.

Overall, the benefits tend to outweigh the challenges, particularly when your family is prepared to appreciate the cross-cultural, observational, social, and linguistic skills developed. Third culture kids also tend to benefit from increased emotional resilience, flexibility, and a fuller perspective. It is encouraging to be aware of the long-term benefits, and making tangible reminders can be a helpful tool.

Activity: The Treasure in the Chest

Objective: To illustrate the way adults and children adapt differently to a new culture and shows benefits of being a TCK.

Materials: Yellow and blue clay (that can be baked to harden); yellow and blue Legos

Description: The mixture of two colors of clay (symbolic of the children) will be contrasted with the mixture of two colors of Legos (symbolic of adults), showing that the children have two culture integrated into their identity that become inseparable, creating a new color, while the distinction between colors in Legos remains clear.

Directions: Take out the yellow and blue Legos. Look at yellow as one culture going into a new, blue culture.

- Blue Legos can be attached to the yellow, but no matter how hard you push them together the colors remain distinct, even if well-built. That is how adults enter a new culture—they can adopt pieces, but still see a clear difference between the two.

- Next take yellow and blue clay, and look at how they can be mixed to varying degrees. Sometimes the colors are very distinct, but well attached, sometimes more swirls, with both colors visible, as well as green appearing. If completely mixed, only the new color of green showing.

- "Third Culture Kids" are not fully the parents' culture (yellow) or the host cultures (blue). A new, unique culture (green) is shared with others who grow up in that mobile, international experience. The "culture" is not from a single color (with more a concrete definition by location or ethnicity). Aspects of the first and second cultures may still be visible, but the distinct lifestyle allows them to best identify with other TCKs.

81

- What does the "yellow" (parents') culture look like right now?

_____

_____

- Often TCKs live in multiple cultures while growing up, with many different shades of blue contributing to the rich cultural experience. What might the "blue" (destination) culture or cultures look like?

_____

_____

- Adults have already developed their main color before moving, but they can still adopt parts of the new culture. Children are still forming the "color" of their cultural identity.
- What parts of the experiences will they share with others that grow up in more than one culture? What makes it a new color?

_____

_____

- It is important to notice that the combination looks different every time, as each person has a unique experience. What are some reasons for these differences?

_____

_____

- Give children both colors of clay, and tell them they can mix it however much they want and make a symbolic object to keep as a reminder. You can also build objects out of Legos, showing the difference of making things from soft or hard material.
- While making the clay objects, talk about the benefits and challenges of growing up in this lifestyle (see Appendix A). How can the experience be used for the best?

_____

_____

- What clay figures did you make? How can they be a reminder of who you are?

_____

_____

_____

_____

_____

_____

_____

_____

How do parents preserve their own culture(s)?

Staying connected with your country is very important on a long-term scale. It allows your children to have a sense of belonging and understanding when going back to your home. That connection is partly through relationships, such as staying in touch with extended family member. Your family can observe and discuss national holidays, and your heritage and history. Doing so will help your children understand events and traditions.

It is also important to keep realistic expectations about what it will look like to go back to your country. This might include differences from what you remember, as nothing remains the same. It helps to stay "up to date" in the changing trends. One way to do that is to sustain a strong relationship with a family with children of similar ages. A long-distance friend or pen-pal can also be someone to connect with when coming back to your country of origin.

Remember that the form of education can be a key factor in how much exposure your children will have to each culture. For example, those in international schools may interact more with Western culture and need to take more initiative to participate in the local culture. Those in a national school may need to be more proactive in maintaining contact with your culture. There isn't one "right" way to do it. All children are unique and will do best in different ways. The key is finding a balance.

Points to Ponder:

Now is a chance to recognize and discuss how the balance between the parents' heritage and the host culture should be maintained.

- Think back to the last activity. Both colors/cultures are important to one's identity and should not be ignored or forgotten.

- Without knowing about the parents' culture, kids will feel even more ignorant and out of place when returning for furlough or permanently.

- There are many ways to stay in touch with that culture. Think of some practical ways to:

    o Keep in touch with relatives:

    _____

    _____

    _____

    o Celebrate national holidays:

    _____

    _____

    _____

    o Learn about the country's history:

    _____

    _____

    _____

    o Maintain awareness of the major events occurring or well-known individuals:

    _____

    _____

    _____

    o Match children with "buddies" or long-distance friends their age who are willing to stay in touch and keep them up-to-date on the latest trends:

_____

_____

_____

o Other ideas:

_____

_____

_____

_____

_____

_____

What's ahead?

No matter how much preparation is done, there are always questions about the upcoming changes. Life is an adventure, and we do not know what will happen until we turn the page. At the same time, it is normal to have hopes and expectations, questions and uncertainties. Some things may go as planned; others might be unexpected. But through it all, your family members have each other, and hopefully have developed ways to offer each other needed love and support. There is always room for growth in relationships, and that growth often happens the most in the midst of challenges.

Activity: A Look Through the Telescope: What's Ahead?

Objective: To help your family think about the long-term aspects of a mobile lifestyle and to practice teamwork, with an opportunity to get excited about the novelty to come and the privilege of experiencing it!

Materials: Varies

Description: Your family will put together a creative representation of what life might be like in five years. This can be done as a skit, song, poem, collage, or another medium.

Directions: When on a ship sometimes telescopes are used to see what's ahead. The farther away something is, the harder it is to see, but if you can see the general shape you can make a guess about what it will look like.

- Pretend that you have a telescope looking toward the future. Brainstorm together about what things might look like in 5 years.

_____

_____

_____

_____

_____

_____

_____

_____

_____

_____

- Think of a way to present what the scene might look like, as if you are allowing someone else to get a glimpse through that telescope.
- You can use any medium you want, such as a recording of acting, singing, or drama, or a form of visual art. This representation can be something to share with others, or to keep and see how accurate it is five years from now.
- Talk about how it feels to look into the future. Are there any fears? Hopes? Goals?

_____

_____

_____

_____

_____

_____

- In what ways can you make sure that you will always provide a constant for each other?

Conclusion

Over the course of the program your family has accumulated a number of tangible and conceptual tools to take with them overseas. The small objects created in activities, such as maps or the radio, can be used by your children to express emotions such as confusion or anxiety, to ask questions about the future or direction, or simply to show a need for a listening ear. These visual representations of activities can later be used as the basis for family conversations concerning the issues addressed, and as reminders to use the skills they have learned. The interactive nature of the program creates memories from which your family can share and learn.

As mentioned in the introduction, this program is in no way comprehensive, but it serves to equip you as a family in ways previously overlooked and provides a basis for areas of future growth. Whether done in a shorter, more intensive timeframe or over an extended period of time, the principles introduced are vital for long-term well-being overseas, both for each individual and for your family as a whole. But even more important than any of the discussions or activities included, is the awareness of the ultimate source of loving unity. Above all else:

Trust in LORD with all your heart and lean not on your own understanding; in all your ways acknowledge him, and he will make your paths straight.

Proverbs 3: 5-6

Appendix A: Third Culture Kids

Benefits and Challenges of Being a TCK
(From Pollock, 2001)

Benefits	Challenges
Growing Up	
• Generally more mature, have had more relationships with adults, causing more sophisticated communication skills • Have learned to be more independent and autonomous because of the nature of mobility	• May feel a little "out of sync" with peers of home culture (e.g. dating, school) • Often experience delayed adolescent rebellion by facing anger and loneliness in college, far from host cultures and family • Tendency to bargain with life, grieving a childhood that cannot be relived
Relationships	
• Able to enter relationships at a deeper and more intimate level because of practice and urgency (knowing the time may be short) • Value relationships • Have a sense of realism about relationships, that grief and loss happens to everyone • Independent and self-reliant, contributing in healthier ways to relationships	• Guarded because of so many lost relationships, may put up boundaries to intimacy, refusing to be vulnerable • May distrust adults, danger of being cynical and mistrusting • Tendency to be emotionally "dull" • Once insulated and self-protected, vulnerable to loneliness
Language	
• Typically speak more than one language, find it easier to learn new languages • Able to appreciate variation in logic and thought present in other languages • Stronger oral and written communication skills • May even have better ability to key into others' learning styles	• Limited in any one language, because not entirely fluent – vocabulary and forms of expression may be incomplete • Find difficulty with phonetics and spelling • May be more easily confused with multiple languages
Worldview	
• Possess a "third dimensional" view, with knowledge, understanding, and empathy for various perspectives on life • Secure in own perspective because it's been "tried and tested" • Motivation to bring about change for the better, to help others (like in relief organizations)	• Feel the pain of reality (such as starvation, poverty, destruction), frustration that others don't share the same world view • Danger of becoming impatient and arrogant with others who have "one dimensional" view of life • May feel confused about where loyalties lie and may be perceived as less patriotic

• Based on experience, realize people around the world are more similar than different	
Cross-Cultural Skills	
• Have learned to be observant, adaptable, flexible, compliant, less judgmental • Capable of mentoring others because life experiences have been so varied	• May be perceived as socially slow because take time to assimilate new surroundings and social mores • Tempted to become "social chameleons" just to fit it • May be less assertive in new situations and perceived as lacking conviction
Cultural Identity	
• Rich cultural background with elements of various cultures internalized • Broad base of knowledge of the world and of people	• "Hidden immigrant," others don't recognize or know your nomadic history • May feel out of balance with home culture, never really feel like you belong • Question values and experience cultural discord • Struggle with unwritten aspects of culture (e.g. history, humor, rules, even trivia), can be a lonely feeling
Mobility	
• Adaptable, flexible • Confident with change even if you don't like it • Sharpened perspective on life and a rich and colorful memory bank • Many and varied relationships and experiences • Recognition that the present time is important and should be lived to the fullest	• Feeling of rootlessness, that "home" is always elsewhere • Migratory instinct, trouble making decisions or staying put with academic choices, career, family, etc. • Try to sustain too many relationships, often around the globe • Difficulty in planning because so many previous decisions have been preempted
Transition (from One Culture to Another)	
• Sensitivity and empathy for others because you've been through transition many times • Know how to put closure on one phase of life and welcome a new one	• Feel like a victim of transition, brush off the pain without dealing with it • Unresolved grief that leads to anger and depression • Relive grief when others experience it, may have own delayed reaction

Appendix B: Resilient Families

Resilience can be defined as "the ability to withstand and rebound from disruptive life challenges."[13] It includes not only surviving difficulties but also adapting and growing, both as individuals and in relationships. This kind of resiliency is key when approaching major life changes such as relocation to a brand new culture.

Overall, John Powell identified seven characteristics of healthy missionary families:

1) Trust: honest interactions, predictability, and kept promises and expectations.
2) Openness: being able to share a whole range of experiences and emotions, while simultaneously respecting appropriate boundaries.
3) Unity: mutual commitment that allows the family as a whole to be greater than the sum of its parts, while still respecting differences.
4) Interdependence: meeting each person's needs, while allowing children to gradually grow in independence.
5) Love: putting each other first and finding ways of giving that can flow over into relationships outside the family as well.
6) Faith: believing and trusting in God; expressed in daily life, on a personal level and as a family.
7) Hope: built on the foundation of faith, keeping Christ as central in the family allows seeing beyond current, at times difficult, circumstances to the hope of eternity.[14]

Froma Walsh outlined another framework for the key processes of family resilience, based primarily on belief systems, organizational patterns, and communication/problem-solving.[15]

Key Processes in Family Resilience

Belief Systems
1. Make Meaning of Adversity
   - View resilience as relationally based vs. "rugged individual"
   - Normalize, contextualize adversity and distress
   - Sense of coherence: crisis as meaningful, comprehensible, manageable challenge
   - Casual/explanatory attributions: How could this happen? What can be done?

2. Positive Outlook
   - Hope, optimistic bias; confidence in overcoming odds
   - Courage and en-*courage*-meant; affirm strengths and focus on potential
   - Active initiative and perseverance (Can-do spirit)
   - Master the possible; accept what can't be changed

---

[13] Walsh, F. (2003). Family resilience: A framework for clinical practice. *Family Process, 42,* p.1
[14] Powell, J. (1998). Family dynamics that affect the MK. In *Raising resilient MKs: Resources for caregivers, parents, and teachers* (pp. 190-195). Colorado Springs, CO: Association of Christian Schools International.
[13] Walsh (2003), p.7.

3. Transcendence and Spirituality
   - Larger values, purpose
   - Spirituality: faith, congregational support, healing rituals
   - Inspiration: envision new possibilities; creative expression; social action
   - Transformation: learning, change, and growth from adversity

Organizational Patterns
4. Flexibility
   - Open to change: rebound, reorganize, adapt to fit new challenges
   - Stability through disruption: continuity, dependability, follow-through
   - Strong authoritative leadership: nurturance, protection, guidance
   - Varied family forms: cooperative parenting/caregiving teams
   - Couple/Co-parent relationship: equal partners

5. Connectedness
   - Mutual support, collaboration, and commitment
   - Respect individual needs, differences, and boundaries
   - Seek reconnection, reconciliation of wounded relationships

6. Social and Economic Resources
   - Mobilize kin, social, and community networks; seek models and mentors
   - Build financial security; balance work/family strains

Communication/Problem-solving
7. Clarity
   - Clear, consistent messages (words and actions)
   - Clarify ambiguous information; truth-seeking/truth-speaking

8. Open Emotional Expression
   - Share range of feelings (joy and pain, hopes and fears)
   - Mutual empathy; tolerance for differences
   - Take responsibility for own feelings, behavior; avoid blaming
   - Pleasurable interactions; humor

9. Collaborative Problem-Solving
   - Creative brainstorming; resourcefulness; seize opportunities
   - Shared decision-making; conflict resolution: negotiation, fairness, reciprocity
   - Focus on goals; take concrete steps; build on success; learn from failure
   - Proactive stance: prevent problems; avert crises; prepare for future challenges

Appendix C: Vulnerability to Stress Scale

Certain aspects of our habits, our lifestyles, and our environments can make each of us more or less vulnerable to the negative effects of stress. How vulnerable are YOU to stress?

Components and variables	Almost always 0 points	Usually 1 point	Sometimes 2 points	Seldom 3 points	Never 4 points
1. I eat at least one hot, balanced meal a day.					
2. I get 7-8 hours of sleep, at least 4 nights a week.					
3. I give and receive affection regularly.					
4. I have at least 1 relative within 50 miles on whom I can rely.					
5. I exercise to the point of perspiration at least twice a week.					
6. I smoke less that half a pack of cigarettes a day (non-smokers = almost always).					
7. I drink fewer than 5 alcoholic drinks a week (non-drinkers = almost always).					
8. I am the appropriate weight for my height.					
9. I have an income adequate to meet my basic needs.					
10. I get strength from my religious/spiritual beliefs.					
11. I regularly attend club or social activities.					
12. I have a network of friends and acquaintances.					
13. I have at least 1 friend in whom I confide about personal matters.					
14. I am in good health (including eyesight, hearing, teeth, etc.).					
15. I am able to speak openly about my feelings when angry or worried.					
16. I have regular conversations with my housemates about domestic problems.					
17. I do something fun at least once a week.					

18. I am able to organize my time effectively.					
19. I drink fewer than 3 caffeine drinks a day.					
20. I take quiet time for myself during the day.					
Total					

0-10 excellent resistance to the vulnerability of stress
11-29 little vulnerability to stress
30-49 some vulnerability to stress
50-74 serious vulnerability
75-80 extreme vulnerability

Source: University of California, Berkeley Wellness Letter, August, 1985. Scale Developers: Lyle Miller, Ph.D. and Alma Dell Smith, Ph.D.

Appendix D: Resources

Books

Families on the Move: Growing Up Overseas - And Loving It!
Knell, M. (2001). Kregel Publications

Fitted Pieces: A Guide for Parents Educating Children Overseas.
Blomberg, J. & Brooks, D. (Eds.) (2001). St Clair Shores, MI: SHARE Education Services

Footsteps Around the World: Relocation Tips for Teens
Roman, B. D. (2000) BR Anchor Publishing

Third Culture Kids: Growing Up Among Worlds
Pollock, D. C., Van Reken, R. E. (2009) Nicholas Brealey Publishing

Where in the World Are You Going?
Blohm, J. M. (1996). Intercultural Press

Web Resources
MKs

Interaction International
Today's Voice for Third Culture Kids and Internationally Mobile Families
http://www.interactionintl.org/home.asp

MK Connection
A central place for finding things of interest to MKs and TCKs.
http://www.mknet.org/

mkPLANET
A growing community designed and run by current missionary kids (MKs) and adult missionary kids (AMKs) as an active community providing information, interaction, and support.
http://www.mkplanet.com/

Mu Kappa
A fraternal association for MKs. A ministry of Barnabas International.
http://mukappa.org/

TCK World
The Official Home of Third Culture Kids
http://www.tckworld.com/

Training

Institute for Cross-Cultural Training (ICCT)
ICCT equips Christians to meet some of the principal challenges of cross-cultural ministry.
http://www.wheaton.edu/bgc/ICCT/

International Training Partners
Provides practical, interactive, biblical training for Christian leaders from around the world, including workshops to enhance ministry effectiveness through improved interpersonal skills and workshops for training facilitators of interactive adult learning.
http://www.relationshipskills.com/

Mission Training International (MTI)
Provides character development training and debriefing on the issues that are very practical and highly relevant to thriving in missions.
http://www.mti.org/homepage.htm

Member Care

Alongside
Alongside is a nonprofit organization whose mission is to provide professional spiritual, mental, and emotional care to missionaries and their families, to the end of promoting personal wholeness and ministry effectiveness.
http://www.alongsidecares.net/

Barnabas International
Barnabas provides pastoral care to missionaries, MKs, global servants and their families.
http://www.barnabas.org/

Caring for Others
Caring for Others is an evangelical Christian ministry committed to helping churches, mission agencies, and other parachurch organizations better care for their members and the people they serve.
http://www.caringforothers.org/

Global Member Care Resources
Provides the global mission/aid community with quality member care materials that inform and equip.
http://www.membercare.org/

Link Care Center
Link Care provides numerous services to missionaries and their organizations. These services range from the Restoration/Personal Growth program, to training and consultation services, to crisis debriefing services.
http://www.linkcare.org/

MemCare by Radio
This is an internet Member Care Resource for those living and working cross-culturally.
http://membercareradio.com/

Missionary Outreach Support Services
An online means of sharing support and resources.
http://missionaryoutreach.net/

Missionary Care
Dr. Ron Koteskey is a Member Care Consultant for New Hope International Ministries. Ron and his wife Bonnie, offer on-field help to independent missionaries, to missionaries whose agencies have no one designated for missionary care.
http://www.missionarycare.com/index.htm

Narramore Christian Foundations
Psychology for Living is a website contains many fine on-line articles dedicated to preventing and solving problems through counseling from a Christian perspective.
http://www.ncfliving.org/

Women of the Harvest
A ministry dedicated to serving and encouraging women in cross-cultural service.
https://www.womenoftheharvest.com/main_nav.asp

Worldwide Families
Worldwide Families offers resources for families currently living or preparing to move overseas.
http://www.worldwidefamilies.org/

For more resources come visit us online!

Worldwide Families
http://www.worldwidefamilies.org/

Worldwide Writings
http://www.worldwidefamilies.org/worldwidewritings/